P9-BBU-033

HOW WE ARE Smart

by W. Nikola-Lisa

illustrated by Sean Qualls

Lee & Low Books Inc. *New York*

To Torre, smart in so many ways—W.N.-L.

To my loving Aunt Fay—S.Q.

Text copyright © 2006 by W. Nikola-Lisa
Illustrations copyright © 2006 by Sean Qualls

All rights reserved. No part of the contents of this book may be reproduced
by any means without the written permission of the publisher.
LEE & LOW BOOKS Inc., 95 Madison Avenue, New York, NY 10016
leeandlow.com

Manufactured in China by Jade Productions, May 2015

Book design by Christy Hale
Book production by The Kids at Our House

The text is set in Sabon, Rockwell, and Franklin Gothic.
The illustrations are rendered in paper, pencil, and acrylic.

HC 10 9 8 7 6 5 4 3 2
PB 10 9 8 7 6 5 4
First Edition

Library of Congress Cataloging-in-Publication Data
Nikola-Lisa, W.
How we are smart / by W. Nikola-Lisa ; illustrated by Sean Qualls.— 1st ed.
p. cm.
Summary: "Through direct quotations, verse, and prose, presents the achievements
of a diverse group of people who illustrate Dr. Howard Gardner's theory of multiple
intelligences. Includes information about the eight basic ways people can be 'smart'
and suggested activities"—Provided by publisher.
ISBN 978-1-58430-254-4 (hc)   ISBN: 978-1-60060-444-7 (pb)
1. Biography—Poetry. 2. Intellect—Poetry. 3. Multiple intelligences—Poetry.
4. Young adult poetry, American. I. Qualls, Sean, ill. II. Title.
PS3564.I375H69 2006
811'.54—dc22   2005015316

Dear Reader,

Think about all the people you know. Are some really good at sports?
Do others excel in art? Can some play musical instruments well? Are some
terrific at solving math problems?

What do all these people have in common? They are smart! But . . . they
are smart in different ways, and in more ways than one. Here are eight
basic ways people can be smart. An explanation of each is given at the
back of the book.

BODY SMART	PEOPLE SMART
LOGIC SMART	PICTURE SMART
MUSIC SMART	SELF SMART
NATURE SMART	WORD SMART

In this book you will meet some fascinating real people, and learn how
they are smart. And then you'll get a chance to figure out all the ways
YOU are smart!

W. Nikola-Lisa
Sean Qualls

LUIS ALVAREZ

The single most important characteristic of my success in physics has been invention. Whenever anything has interested me, I have instinctively tried to invent a new or better way of doing it.

PHYSICIST LUIS ALVAREZ

Have you heard about Luis
and his studious ways?
He thought learning was fun
from his earliest days.
He read about atoms.
He thought about quarks.
He studied the universe
and how it all works.
He asked lots of questions.
Most scientists do.
Like what is a star?
And why is there flu?
Luis thought and studied;
that's how he was reared.
He even figured out how
the dinosaurs disappeared.
Yes, Luis was smart—
so curious and inventive;
the way he solved problems
was wonderfully creative.
Are you smart like Luis?

LUIS ALVAREZ (1911–1988), of Spanish and Irish ancestry, was the son of a medical researcher. As a boy Luis was fascinated by how things worked, and at age eleven, with the help of his father, he built his own radio. In college Luis studied experimental physics, an area of science that develops new technologies. As a physicist he worked on radar landing systems, the atomic bomb, and the detection of subatomic particles. With his son, a geologist, Luis correctly proposed that severe changes in Earth's climate due to the impact of a large meteorite were responsible for the disappearance of the dinosaurs sixty-five million years ago.

MARIA TALLCHIEF

As a little girl, I didn't have much time to dream. . . . Most of my day was taken up with schoolwork, and music and ballet lessons.

BALLERINA MARIA TALLCHIEF

Here comes Maria
   to take center stage.
   It's a place she craved
   from a tender young age.
For Maria loved to dance,
   to leap, and to soar;
   to spring toward the sky;
   to fly across the floor.
She could have been a singer—
   a clear-throated soprano—
   or a professional musician
   playing concert piano.
But dance was what she lived for.
   Dance was who she was.
   And when Maria took flight
   the audience was a-buzz.
Yes, Maria was smart—
   so incredibly dignified;
   she used movement to show
   what she felt deep inside.
Are you smart like Maria?

MARIA TALLCHIEF (b. 1925), of Osage Indian and Scotch-Irish ancestry, is regarded as America's first prima ballerina. She was the first lead dancer of a ballet company born, raised, and trained in the United States. Maria's interest in dancing began as a child watching the Osage ceremonial dances. Soon ballet captured her heart, and she began studying with the legendary Russian teacher Bronislava Nijinska. At seventeen, Maria moved to New York City to join the Ballet Russe de Monte Carlo. She later became a principal dancer for the New York City Ballet under the direction of the famous choreographer George Balanchine, who created several ballets just for her.

THURGOOD MARSHALL

*My commitments have always been justice for all people,
regardless of race, creed, or color.*

JUSTICE THURGOOD MARSHALL

Hats off to Thurgood,
    good-natured and kind,
    who listened to everyone
    with his razor-sharp mind.
He thought about people.
    He thought about law.
    He thought about everything
    he witnessed and saw.
He stood up to lawyers,
    no matter their wealth.
    He stood up to judges,
    though a judge himself.
He stood up for freedom,
    for the poor and oppressed;
    and when he stood up,
    the world was impressed.
Yes, Thurgood was smart—
    he reached for great heights,
    used the power of the courts
    to protect people's rights.
Are you smart like Thurgood?

THURGOOD MARSHALL (1908–1993), great-grandson of a slave and son of a railroad dining-car waiter, had a long career as a lawyer, civil rights activist, and judge. He joined the National Association for the Advancement of Colored People (NAACP) as a young man and for twenty-three years directed its legal department. In 1954 he won one of the most important legal cases of the twentieth century, *Brown v. Board of Education,* which ended the segregation of black people in schools and other public facilities. In 1967 Thurgood became the first African American Supreme Court Justice, a position he held for twenty-four years until his retirement in 1991.

ANNIE JUMP CANNON

My success, if you would call it that, lies in the fact that I have kept at my work all these years. It is not genius or anything like that, it is merely patience.

ASTRONOMER ANNIE JUMP CANNON

I'd like you to meet Annie,
  whose lifelong love
  was studying the stars
  and the night sky above.
As a young girl she huddled
  with her mother at night
  to study the stars and
  their astonishing light.
She went on to college
  in search of a path;
  she'd always liked science,
  especially math.
We know Annie most
  for her quick, keen eye
  as she sorted the stars
  by their light in the sky.
Yes, Annie was smart—
  painstakingly exact;
  through patience and discipline
  she made a big impact.
Are you smart like Annie?

ANNIE JUMP CANNON (1863–1941), of Scottish descent, was the daughter of a Delaware shipbuilder. Her interest in astronomy was sparked by her mother, who taught Annie about the star constellations. In college she studied math, physics, and astronomy, and in 1896 Annie joined the Harvard College Observatory. During the next forty years, she classified more than 350,000 stars using the technique of spectroscopy, a photographic process that shows the different bands of light produced by stars. She also refined the Harvard College star classification system, which is still in use today. In 1931 Annie became the first woman awarded the National Academy of Sciences' Draper Gold Medal.

TITO PUENTE

*My mother put me to study immediately because they saw that
I had a lot of talent musically. . . . I was always banging around
cans and the walls and doing a lot of percussion things.*

MUSICIAN TITO PUENTE

Let's read about Tito
    who through his fame
    made Latin music
    a household name.
He played like no other,
    with energy and drive,
    ***thump-thumping* his drums,**
    dancing them alive.
He played bongos, congas,
    timbales, and vibraphone;
    he played them with gusto
    and exceptional tone.
He toured the world
    to thunderous ovations;
    the King of Latin Music
    touched all generations.
Yes, Tito was smart—
    musically so gifted,
    when he began to play
    hearts were uplifted.
Are you smart like Tito?

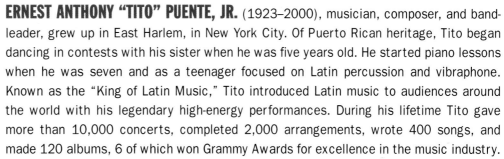

ERNEST ANTHONY "TITO" PUENTE, JR. (1923–2000), musician, composer, and band-leader, grew up in East Harlem, in New York City. Of Puerto Rican heritage, Tito began dancing in contests with his sister when he was five years old. He started piano lessons when he was seven and as a teenager focused on Latin percussion and vibraphone. Known as the "King of Latin Music," Tito introduced Latin music to audiences around the world with his legendary high-energy performances. During his lifetime Tito gave more than 10,000 concerts, completed 2,000 arrangements, wrote 400 songs, and made 120 albums, 6 of which won Grammy Awards for excellence in the music industry.

PATSY TAKEMOTO MINK

There is no doubt that for me the turning point in my life was having the opportunity to attend law school and to become an attorney. It opened all the doors that previously had been shut.

CONGRESSWOMAN PATSY TAKEMOTO MINK

Come listen to Patsy
    and her inspiring ways,
    who fought for justice
    throughout her days.
A teacher, a lawyer,
    a mother, a politician:
    whatever she did,
    she did with conviction.
She championed causes for
    the downtrodden and poor.
    She stood up for women
    to help them achieve more.
She was warm and friendly,
    without a trace of guile;
    but she got things done
    with her no-nonsense style.
Yes, Patsy was smart—
    spirited and forthright;
    she worked to help people
    improve their plight.
Are you smart like Patsy?

PATSY TAKEMOTO MINK (1927–2002), a third-generation Japanese American, was born into a Maui, Hawaii, sugar plantation community. As a child she wanted to become a doctor, but few medical schools admitted women. A friend suggested she study to be a lawyer instead. After a few years practicing law, Patsy ran for public office and was elected to the House of Representatives, becoming the first woman of color in the U.S. Congress. She fought for the rights of minorities, the poor, women, and children, and was reelected twelve times. Patsy is best known for her support of legislation that requires equal promotion of women's sports at colleges.

MATTHEW HENSON

The great accomplishments of the world have been achieved by men who had . . . great visions. The path is not easy, the climbing is rugged and hard, but the glory at the end is worthwhile.

EXPLORER MATTHEW HENSON

Do you know Matthew,
   who loved open spaces,
   ocean spray, fresh air,
   and faraway places?
He cared not for cities,
   where he never felt free,
   so he packed up his bags
   and shipped out to sea.
To the top of the world,
   to the North Pole he went,
   where ice froze his fingers
   and wind slashed his tent.
But Matthew never faltered.
   He kept pushing on
   until he came to that place
   no explorer had ever gone.
Yes, Matthew was smart—
   so practical yet bold;
   he braved nature's fury,
   endured bitter cold.
Are you smart like Matthew?

MATTHEW HENSON (1866–1955) was born to free African American parents. Orphaned as a young boy, he went to sea as a cabin boy at age thirteen. For the remainder of his teenage years, he traveled the world. In 1887 Robert Peary, then a U.S. Navy engineer, hired Matthew as his assistant. They sailed together for the next twenty years, first looking for the best location to build a canal to connect the Atlantic and Pacific oceans and then searching for the geographic North Pole. On April 6, 1909, after several trips to the Arctic, Henson and Peary became the first explorers to reach the North Pole.

GEORGIA O'KEEFFE

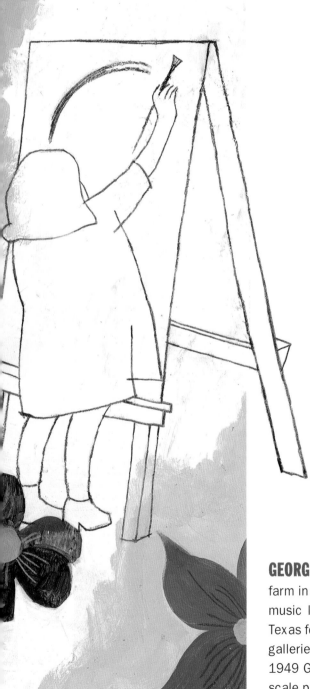

I asked our washwoman's daughter what she was going to do when she grew up. She said she didn't know. I said very definitely, . . . "I'm going to be an artist."

ARTIST GEORGIA O'KEEFFE

How about Georgia,
    who right from the start
    yearned to paint pictures,
    longed to make art.
A sky filled with clouds.
    A white trumpet flower.
    A sun-bleached bone.
    A lonely desert bower.
These are the things
    Georgia saw each day.
    These are the things
    Georgia painted her way.
Color and form—that's
    what caught her eye—
    color and form and
    that Southwestern sky.
Yes, Georgia was smart—
    sensitive and aware;
    her world the inspiration
    for paintings truly rare.
Are you smart like Georgia?

GEORGIA O'KEEFFE (1887–1986), the daughter of Irish immigrants, grew up on a dairy farm in Wisconsin. To supplement her public school education, Georgia received art and music lessons at home. After studying in Chicago and New York, and teaching art in Texas for several years, Georgia began painting full time and exhibiting her work in major galleries. Her paintings were very personal, expressing her own ideas and feelings. In 1949 Georgia moved to New Mexico, where she lived for the rest of her life. Her large-scale paintings of desert rocks, plants, bones, and flowers established her as one of the most important twentieth-century American artists.

ALEXANDER POSEY

The Indian talks in . . . the free and untrammeled poetry of Nature, the poetry of the fields, the sky, the river, the sun and stars. In his own tongue it is not difficult for the Indian to compose.

POET ALEXANDER POSEY

Here comes Alexander,
   full of cunning and wit,
   and strength of character
   that showed real grit.
He wrote about the people,
   of the Muscogee nation.
   He wrote about their lives
   from their earliest creation.
He was wonderfully insightful,
   wise beyond his years.
   He understood his people
   and helped voice their fears.
He created lasting characters,
   like Chinnubbie Harjo,
   who enabled his people
   to laugh at their sorrow.
Yes, Alexander was smart—
   so funny and clever;
   his innovative words
   will endure forever.
Are you smart like Alexander?

ALEXANDER L. POSEY (1873–1908), the son of a Creek (Muscogee) mother and a Scotch-Irish father, was a happy, carefree child who spoke both Creek and English. An eager student, Alexander attended Indian University in Bacone, Oklahoma, graduating in 1895. He was a poet, journalist, educator, and longtime editor of the *Indian Journal*, an influential newspaper that addressed economic and political issues facing the native peoples of Oklahoma Territory in the late 1800s. Considered one of the most important Indian writers of his time, Alexander's writing was fresh, humorous, and original, often taking the form of witty conversations between invented Native American characters.

MARIAN ANDERSON

When the day came for our class to go [to singing class], I was the happiest child in the school. I knew every song. . . . I just put back my head and sang as loudly as I could.

SINGER MARIAN ANDERSON

Marian we remember
    for the singing she did;
    and she started so young,
    just a fun-loving kid.
She sang hymns at church.
    She sang songs in school.
    Music was her trade,
    voice her chosen tool.
But it wasn't always easy,
    there were still things to face;
    some doors slammed shut
    on account of her race.
But Marian persisted
    until the world was her stage:
    from New York to Paris,
    Marian was the rage!
Yes, Marian was smart—
    gracious yet compelling;
    her voice like a waterfall,
    powerfully overwhelming.
Are you smart like Marian?

MARIAN ANDERSON (1897–1993) grew up in a close-knit African American family in Philadelphia, where she began singing with a church choir and later with the Philadelphia Choral Society. After winning a local competition in 1925, Marian appeared as a soloist with the New York Philharmonic Orchestra and then began to tour extensively. In 1939 she was barred from singing at Constitution Hall in Washington, D. C., because she was black. Instead, Marian gave a concert on the steps of the Lincoln Memorial for thousands of admirers. Known for her rich, velvety voice, Marian was the first African American to sing at the Metropolitan Opera in New York City.

I. M. PEI

When I first started my practice, I did draw a lot. Very quickly afterwards I found that I could draw faster in my head than I could draw on paper.

ARCHITECT I. M. PEI

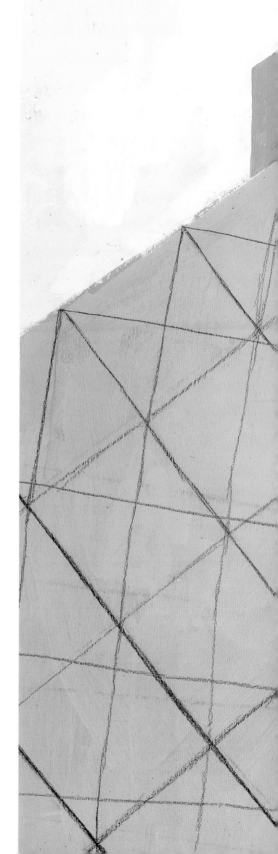

Have you heard of I. M.,
　　who saw soaring spaces,
　　towering steel buildings
　　in all sorts of places?
As a youngster he knew
　　it was buildings he'd design
　　with the intricate geometries
　　of shape, form, and line.
His buildings are crisp,
　　clear, and detailed;
　　that's why his ideas
　　have long been hailed.
From soaring interiors
　　to walls of sheer glass
　　to banded steel girders
　　that carry the mass.
Yes, I. M. was smart—
　　passionate and devoted;
　　his ideas for new projects
　　wholeheartedly promoted.
Are you smart like I. M.?

IEOH MING "I. M." PEI (b. 1917) has designed buildings all over the world. Born in China, he came to the United States at seventeen to study architecture. Whether he is designing skyscrapers, libraries, schools, hospitals, or performing arts centers, I. M. tries to integrate the structure of a building into its surrounding environment. Two of his most important projects include the East Wing of the National Gallery of Art in Washington, D. C., and the Glass Pyramid visitor entrance to the Louvre Museum in Paris, France. I. M. has received many awards for his work, including the prestigious Pritzker Architecture Prize and the National Medal of Arts.

YNÉS MEXÍA

I am not a dyed-in-the-wool scientist, I am a nature lover and a bit of an adventuress, and my collecting is secondary, even though very real and very important.

BOTANIST YNÉS MEXÍA

Let's read about Ynés,
   who really liked to travel,
   not on super highways
   but on roads of dirt and gravel.
She fell in love with nature,
   left her California home;
   taking just what she needed,
   she set off to roam.
She traveled to Central America
   and South America too.
   She climbed ancient ruins,
   sailed the Amazon to Peru.
For thirteen exciting years
   she collected native plants,
   dodging local bandits
   and foraging fire ants.
Yes, Ynés was smart—
   her persistence contagious;
   in wild, faraway places,
   her devotion courageous.
Are you smart like Ynés?

YNÉS MEXÍA (1870–1938), of Mexican American heritage, endured much unhappiness early in life—her parents' divorce, her father's untimely death, two short-lived marriages. Finally, at age forty, she moved to California, joined a hiking club, and fell in love with nature. After studying botany as a special college student, Ynés began to lead expeditions. She collected plants from the slopes of Mount McKinley in Alaska to the rain forests of Brazil, often camping in dangerous conditions. After each trip she returned to California to sort, identify, mount, and photograph her specimens. Ynés amassed a collection of close to 145,000 plants, including some species she discovered herself.

Eight Ways to Be Smart

In the opening letter we mentioned that there are eight ways to be smart. This idea, or theory, is called "multiple intelligences." It was developed by Dr. Howard Gardner, a psychologist at Harvard University, and popularized by Dr. Thomas Armstrong, an educator and psychologist.

Everyone is smart in his or her own way, and each of us uses all eight intelligences to some degree. Here is information about the traits, interests, and activities most often associated with each way of being smart. You'll see there are lots of different ways to express each intelligence.

—W.N.-L. and S.Q.

BODY SMART People who are body smart use their bodies to solve problems or communicate ideas that cannot be expressed in other ways. They are usually physically coordinated and strong. Dancers, actors, athletes, mechanics, builders, surgeons, and sculptors are all body smart. If *you* are body smart you might like to use your body to express yourself, enjoy moving your body, or be good at many physical activities.

LOGIC SMART People who are logic smart can solve complex problems using either language or numbers. They have the ability to notice patterns and approach problems logically. Mathematicians, scientists, computer programmers, lawyers, writers, and engineers are all logic smart. If *you* are logic smart you might be good with numbers, ask lots of questions, enjoy figuring out things you don't understand, or like to do experiments.

MUSIC SMART People who are music smart like music, of course, and they are very aware of nonverbal sounds in their surroundings. They have a knack for remembering melodies, noticing pitches and rhythms, and keeping time. Singers, musicians, composers, sound engineers, and songwriters are all music smart. If *you* are music smart you might like to hum tunes, sing songs, listen to music, or play an instrument.

NATURE SMART People who are nature smart recognize features in the natural world, enjoy classifying things, and understand the environment. They are sensitive to nature and how the activities of people affect the natural world. Animal trainers, gardeners, explorers, environmentalists, and landscapers are all nature smart. If *you* are nature smart you might like to take walks, garden, care for pets and animals, or just gaze up at the sky.

PEOPLE SMART People who are people smart are aware of the moods, feelings, and desires of others. They care about people and can work effectively with them. Teachers, coaches, doctors, politicians, salespeople, and religious leaders are all people smart. If *you* are people smart, you might know many people, enjoy being with them, or have lots of friends. You might like working in groups, often becoming the leader.

PICTURE SMART People who are picture smart think in pictures, creating mental images or models of what they are thinking about. They tend to remember things in images instead of words. Artists, architects, inventors, interior decorators, some scientists, and land surveyors are all picture smart. If *you* are picture smart you might like to draw or paint; enjoy working puzzles and mazes; or be good at reading maps, diagrams, and graphs.

SELF SMART People who are self smart have good knowledge of their strengths and weaknesses. They learn from their experiences, set personal goals, and are sensitive to their own feelings and those of others. Actors, film makers, clergy members, writers, and guidance counselors are all self smart. If *you* are self smart you might like to keep a diary or journal, create your own projects and activities, or solve problems by yourself.

WORD SMART People who are word smart like to use words. They possess a love of and a facility with spoken and written language, and have an ability to learn languages. Poets, writers, lawyers, journalists, politicians, comedians, and speechwriters are all word smart. If *you* are word smart you might be good at memorizing names, places, and dates; reading, writing, and telling stories; or learning foreign languages.

How We Are Smart

Now it's time for you to think about the ways we are smart, what interests people most—nature, science, music, art?

The twelve people in this book came from many different backgrounds. They had varying interests and talents. They were all smart in different ways, and each person was an individual blend of several intelligences. Maria Tallchief, for example, is a great dancer and also very talented musically. I. M. Pei designs buildings by drawing upon his understanding of nature in addition to applying his vast knowledge of building materials. Marian Anderson had both a great voice and lots of self-esteem, which enabled her to succeed in the face of racial prejudice and discrimination.

ACTIVITIES

Have fun applying what you've read about the ways people can be smart. You'll learn more about the people in this book, and also discover some new and exciting things about yourself, your family, and your friends. Here are a few things for you to try.

▶ Reread the profiles of the people in this book and make a list of the ways you think each person was smart. Then research more information about a few of the people who interest you the most. (You might find out that Thurgood Marshall was also a wonderful storyteller, or that Annie Jump Cannon was also a great dancer!) Look to see how the people you study were smart in ways other than those mentioned in the book.

▶ Choose a topic you want to know more about and read as much as you can on the subject. When you're ready, select one of the eight intelligences and use it to create a "report" about what you've learned. For example, if you choose *picture smart* you might use pictures, charts, diagrams, cartoons, and/or photographs to create your report. If you choose *word smart* you could write a poem, a legend or myth, or even a short story to make your report.

▶ Take some time to observe people around you. Look at your friends, family, or others in your neighborhood. What kinds of things are these people good at? What do they enjoy doing the most? What else do you notice about the person who is a whiz at everything having to do with computers? Is he or she good at anything else? Write down your thoughts and share them with the people you observed. Tell them how you think they are smart!

▶ Think about your own strengths and interests. What do you like to do? What are you good at? What do you know a lot about? Are you smart like some of the people you read about? Write down all the ways you are smart. You may wish to record your thoughts in a journal and then discuss them with your family and/or teachers. Talk about how to develop or improve the ways you are smart. Who knows, maybe one day you'll be in a book like this!

FURTHER READING

Armstrong, Thomas. *You're Smarter Than You Think: A Kid's Guide to Multiple Intelligences.* Minneapolis: Free Spirit, 2003.

Arnold, Ellen. *MI Strategies for Kids.* 7 book set. Chicago: Zephyr Press, 2001.

Resources for Educators, Parents, and Caregivers

BOOKS

Armstrong, Thomas. *In Their Own Way: Discovering and Encouraging Your Child's Multiple Intelligences.* New York: Tarcher, 2000.

———. *Multiple Intelligences in the Classroom.* 2nd ed. Alexandria, VA: Association for Supervision & Curriculum Development, 2000.

———. *The Multiple Intelligences of Reading and Writing: Making the Words Come Alive.* Alexandria, VA: Association for Supervision & Curriculum Development, 2003.

———. *7 Kinds of Smart: Discovering and Identifying Your Multiple Intelligences,* Rev. and updated ed. New York: Plume, 1999.

Baum, Susan, Julie Viens, and Barbara Slatin. *Multiple Intelligences in the Elementary Classroom: A Teacher's Toolkit.* New York: Teachers College Press, 2005.

The Best of Multiple Intelligences Activities from Teacher Created Materials. Westminster, CA: Teacher Created Resources, 1999.

Campbell, Linda, and Bruce Campbell. *Multiple Intelligences and Student Achievement: Success Stories from Six Schools.* Alexandria, VA: Association for Supervision & Curriculum Development, 1999.

DeAmicis, Bonita. *Multiple Intelligences Made Easy.* Chicago: Zephyr Press, 2003.

Gardner, Howard. *Frames of Mind: The Theory of Multiple Intelligences.* New York: Basic Books, 1993.

———. *Intelligence Reframed: Multiple Intelligences for the 21st Century.* New York: Basic Books, 1999.

———. *Multiple Intelligences: The Theory in Practice.* New York: Basic Books, 1993.

Hoerr, Thomas R. *Becoming a Multiple Intelligences School.* Alexandria, VA: Association for Supervision & Curriculum Development, 2000.

Kagan, Spencer, and Miguel Kagan. *The Complete MI Book.* San Clemente, CA: Kagan Cooperative Learning, 1998.

Lazear, David. *Eight Ways of Knowing: Teaching for Multiple Intelligences.* Thousand Oaks, CA: Corwin Press, 1999.

———. *Eight Ways of Teaching: The Artistry of Teaching with Multiple Intelligences.* Thousand Oaks, CA: Corwin Press, 2003.

———. *The Intelligent Curriculum: Using Multiple Intelligences to Develop Your Students' Full Potential.* Chicago: Zephyr Press, 1999.

———. *Multiple Intelligence Approaches to Assessment: Solving the Assessment Conundrum.* Chicago: Zephyr Press, 1998.

Nicholson-Nelson, Kristen. *Developing Students' Multiple Intelligences: Grades K–8.* New York: Scholastic, 1999.

Schiller, Pam, and Pat Phipps. *The Complete Daily Curriculum for Early Childhood: Over 1200 Easy Activities to Support Multiple Intelligences and Learning Styles.* New York: Gryphon House, 2002.

VIDEOS

Armstrong, Thomas. *Multiple Intelligences: Discovering the Giftedness in ALL.* VHS. Port Chester, NY: National Professional Resources, 1997.

———. *The Multiple Intelligences of Reading and Writing: Making the Words Come Alive Books-in-Action Video.* VHS. Alexandria, VA: Association for Supervision & Curriculum Development, 2003.

Gardner, Howard. *How Are Kids Smart? Multiple Intelligences in the Classroom.* VHS. Port Chester, NY: National Professional Resources, 1995.

———. *Multiple Intelligences: Intelligence, Understanding, and the Mind.* 2 VHS. Port Chester, NY: National Professional Resources, 2000.

———, Daniel Goldman, and Mihaly Csikszentmihaly. *Optimizing Intelligences: Thinking, Emotion & Creativity.* VHS. Port Chester, NY: National Professional Resources, 1998.

Hoerr, Thomas R. *Becoming a Multiple Intelligences School Books-in-Action Video.* VHS. Alexandria, VA: Association for Supervision & Curriculum Development, 2000.

WEB SITES

Armstrong, Thomas. Features the work of Dr. Armstrong, an educator and psychologist instrumental in making accessible Dr. Howard Gardner's work on MI theory and its applications to the classroom.
http://thomasarmstrong.com

Gardner, Howard. Features the work of Dr. Gardner and provides helpful tips on how to find out more about MI theory and its implications for education.
http://howardgardner.com

Infed. Provides background information on Dr. Howard Gardner, the development of multiple intelligences theory, and its implications for the classroom.
http://www.infed.org/thinkers/gardner.htm

Lamb, Annette, and Larry Johnson. Features suggestions of ways to incorporate multiple intelligences theory in a technology-rich environment with links to student projects, lesson plans, and MI inventories.
http://eduscapes.com

Lazear, David. Offers workshops, newsletters, reports, and books as well as lesson plans for implementing MI theory in the classroom.
http://www.multi-intell.com

Multiple Intelligences Reading List. A comprehensive list of MI resources from Connecticut's Special Education Resource Center (SERC).
http://www.ctserc.org/library/Articles/Bibliographies.shtml

New Horizons for Learning. An international educational network featuring innovative learning, including information on applying MI theory to the classroom.
http://newhorizons.org/strategies/front_strategies.html

ACKNOWLEDGMENTS

The idea for this book came from the writings of Harvard psychologist Dr. Howard Gardner, whose theory of multiple intelligences I first learned about as a graduate student in the mid-1980s. I am also grateful to Dr. Thomas Armstrong, whose recent writings on MI theory have made Dr. Gardner's ideas accessible to many teachers and parents. The eight terms I use to describe Dr. Gardner's intelligences—body smart, self smart, word smart, and so on—come directly from Dr. Armstrong's writings.

—W.N.-L.

AUTHOR'S SOURCES

Allison, Amy. *Luis Alvarez and the Bubble Chamber.* Hockessin, DE: Mitchell Lane, 2002.

Alvarez, Luis W. *Alvarez: Adventures of a Physicist.* New York: Basic Books, 1987.

Anderson, Marian. *My Lord, What a Morning: An Autobiography.* New York: Viking Penguin, 2002.

Armentrout, David, and Patricia Armentrout. *Matthew Henson: Discover the Life of an American Legend.* Vero Beach, FL: Rourke, 2003.

Bonta, Marcia M., ed. *American Women Afield: Writings by Pioneering Women Naturalists.* College Station, TX: Texas A&M University Press, 1995.

Dolan, Jr., Edward F. *Matthew Henson, Black Explorer.* New York: Dodd, Mead, 1979.

Ferris, Jeri. *Arctic Explorer: The Story of Matthew Henson.* Minneapolis: Carolrhoda, 1990.

Freedman, Russell. *The Voice That Challenged a Nation: Marian Anderson and the Struggle for Equal Rights.* New York: Clarion Books, 2004.

Haskins, Jim. *One More River to Cross: The Stories of Twelve Black Americans.* New York: Scholastic, 1994.

Kass-Simon, G., and Patricia Farnes, eds. *Women of Science: Righting the Record.* Bloomington: Indiana University Press, 1993.

Kosmider, Alexia. *Tricky Tribal Discourse: The Poetry, Short Stories, and Fus Fixico Letters of Creek Writer Alex Posey.* Moscow: University of Idaho Press, 1998.

Littlefield, Jr., Daniel F. *Alex Posey: Creek Poet, Journalist, and Humorist.* Lincoln: University of Nebraska Press, 1992.

———, and C. P. Hunter, eds. *Alexander Posey, The Fus Fixico Letters.* Lincoln: University of Nebraska Press, 1993.

Loza, Steven. *Tito Puente and the Making of Latin Music.* Urbana and Chicago: University of Illinois Press, 1999.

Matsuda, Mari J. *Called from Within: Early Women Lawyers of Hawaii.* Honolulu: University of Hawaii Press, 1992.

McLoone, Margo. *Women Explorers in North and South America.* Mankato, MN: Capstone Press, 1997.

Neuman, Nancy M. *True to Ourselves: A Celebration of Women Making a Difference.* San Francisco: Jossey-Bass, 1998.

O'Keeffe, Georgia. *Georgia O'Keeffe: A Studio Book.* New York: Viking, 1976.

Peyer, Bernd C., ed. *The Singing Spirit: Early Short Stories by North American Indians.* Tucson: University of Arizona Press, 1989.

Polk, Milbry, and Mary Tiegreen. *Women of Discovery: A Celebration of Intrepid Women Who Explored the Earth.* New York: Clarkson Potter, 2001.

Posey, Alexander Lawrence. *The Poems of Alexander Lawrence Posey, Creek Indian Bard.* Muskogee, OK: Hoffman Printing, 1969.

Reynolds, Moira Davison. *American Women Scientists: 23 Inspiring Biographies, 1900–2000.* Jefferson, NC: McFarland, 2004.

Robinson, Roxana. *Georgia O'Keeffe: A Life.* Hanover, NH: University Press of New England, 1999.

Salazar, Max. *Mambo Kingdom: Latin Music in New York.* New York: Schirmer Books, 2003.

Stille, Darlene R. *Extraordinary Women Scientists.* Danbury, CT: Children's Press, 1995.

Tallchief, Maria, with Larry Kaplan. *Maria Tallchief: America's Prima Ballerina.* New York: Henry Holt, 1997.

Tinling, Marion. *Women Into the Unknown: A Sourcebook on Women Explorers and Travelers.* Westport, CT: Greenwood Press, 1989.

Tushnet, Mark V., ed. *Thurgood Marshall: His Speeches, Writings, Arguments, Opinions, and Reminiscences.* Chicago: Lawrence Hill, 2001.

Veglahn, Nancy J. *Women Scientists.* New York: Facts on File, 1991.

von Boehm, Gero. *Conversations with I. M. Pei: Light is the Key.* Munich, Germany: Prestel Verlag, 2000.

Williams, Juan. *Thurgood Marshall: American Revolutionary.* New York: Three Rivers Press, 2000.

Wiseman, Carter. *I. M. Pei: A Profile in American Architecture.* New York: Harry N. Abrams, 2001.

Yost, Edna. *American Women of Science.* Philadelphia: Lippincott, 1955.